THE
MAISTER

A FAMILY TERRORISED BY A FATHER'S CRUELTY

JEAN SCOTT BORTHWICK

THE
MAISTER

A FAMILY TERRORISED BY A FATHER'S CRUELTY

JEAN SCOTT BORTHWICK

MEREO
Cirencester

Mereo Books

1A The Wool Market Dyer Street Cirencester Gloucestershire GL7 2PR
An imprint of Memoirs Publishing www.mereobooks.com

The Maister: 978-1-86151-466-0

First published in Great Britain in 2015
by Mereo Books, an imprint of Memoirs Publishing

The address for Memoirs Publishing Group Limited can be found at
www.memoirspublishing.com

The Memoirs Publishing Group Ltd Reg. No. 7834348

The Memoirs Publishing Group supports both The Forest Stewardship Council® (FSC®) and
the PEFC® leading international forest-certification organisations. Our books carrying both the
FSC label and the PEFC® and are printed on FSC®-certified paper. FSC® is the only
forest-certification scheme supported by the leading environmental organisations including
Greenpeace. Our paper procurement policy can be found at
www.memoirspublishing.com/environment

Typeset in 12/18pt Plantin
by Wiltshire Associates Publisher Services Ltd. Printed and bound in Great Britain by
Printondemand-Worldwide, Peterborough PE2 6XD

CONTENTS

Chapter 1 - Page 1

Chapter 2 - Page 13

Chapter 3 - Page 21

Chapter 4 - Page 33

Chapter 5 - Page 56

Chapter 6 - Page 61

Chapter 7 - Page 71

CHAPTER ONE

The earliest memory I have is of sailing the seven seas with my baby brother Roly in my arms. Our boat was an old wooden wash tub. I was three years old and Roly about eighteen months.

It seems to me now that the sun always shone back then, and we seemed to spend every day in our boat, laughing. Meanwhile my mother and our neighbour Mrs Calder were doing laundry in the washhouse. They had the door wide open and were talking and laughing and keeping an eye on us in our boat.

Also looking into our back yard was the kitchen window of our neighbour Mrs Gourlay, who had a budgie. We would pick "rats' tails" (weeds) for Joey and hand them over the window sill to Mrs Gourlay. She was the local midwife and "layer out" and had remedies for all ills. She was always smiling, as I remember.

My little brother Roly was usually a wriggler and wouldn't settle for long, but he loved to be in the boat with me and I made up stories about where we were going. He would happily try and repeat what I told him, though nobody could make out what he was saying.

"Where will we go today, Roly?"

"Brrrm brrrm." Roly didn't mind where we went. The sun shone on his glorious red hair and it seemed the world was at our feet.

I remember one day we were given an orange to share. An orange! Goodness, we had never seen such a thing. This was 1945 and everything was scarce. How we enjoyed it!

How happy we were, it seems to me now. We didn't have very much in material terms, but we had our little cottage and we had each other. Sometimes we would have a picnic. This would be out in the country beside a burn. We had a huge pram with space under the mattress for sandwiches and tea. Roly had pride of place under the hood and I sat at his feet.

I learned long after that Mother had managed to get this pram second-hand from a friend who could "get anything within reason", although there were none to be had in the shops. It truly was a monster and took up plenty of space in our kitchen.

"You didn't enquire too closely where things came from," she said with a smile. "You were just grateful to have anything."

It seemed to us that we had everything, then.

★ ★ ★

My mother's mother was raped as a young teenager while she was collecting insurance payments during the Great War. At least, that is all I ever learned about my mother's beginnings. This was a dreadful disgrace at that time, both for the mother and (so very unfairly) for the child.

My grandmother (I will call her Lizzie) had a brother who worked in a bank in Edinburgh and was married to a primary school teacher. They were childless, though I believe there had been a damaging miscarriage early in their marriage. They took Lizzie in until her baby was born and for a little while after. I am unclear about what arrangements there were, official or otherwise, to take care of the child. My mother always knew who her natural mother was and called her uncle and aunt Muncle and Mantie thereafter.

Whatever was agreed, my mother was brought up in

their household. Also in the house, which was quite small, was Mantie's mother, whom my mother always referred to as M'granny, and who was good to her. In fact I was named after her. Mantie and Muncle appear to have been cold, selfish people who constantly reminded my poor mother how grateful she should be to them.

Lizzie married at the end of the Great War. Long after, I was told that Bill, her husband, brought ten shillings every week in the train from Edinburgh to pay for my mother's keep. And although he was a casualty of war, having lost a lung, they took it.

M'Granny died when Mum was about 16, I think, and because Mantie was still teaching, a housekeeper was installed. This was our beloved Auntie Bea, whose own mother had just died and whose fiancé had been killed at Mons.

Mother did well at school and went on to Edinburgh University, studying for an MA in maths. At some point during her three years at university, she met my father. Roderick was one of five brothers from the far north of Scotland. This would be around 1935/36. He was also studying for an MA, in languages and classics.

Life on my father's parents' croft must have been hard. His mother bore five sons and a much longed-for daughter, Maggie. There was little money and a lot of hard work. My grandfather was a hard, demanding man, whose own father had been the very devil, I was told.

When Maggie was four years old, she contracted meningitis and died. How truly terrible for my granny, the only daughter who would have been such a help to her, taken cruelly away. My father was only a baby when this happened, and could scarcely remember Maggie.

★ ★ ★

Both my parents duly graduated, went on to teacher training college and became teachers. I gather they had an on/off relationship just before war broke out in 1939.

For some reason, although teaching was a reserved occupation, Father enlisted soon after hostilities began. He joined the army as a Royal Artillery gunner. Just before he was sent away, he asked my mother to marry him and they became engaged. They married quietly in April 1941.

At that time Mother was teaching away from home, but after the wedding she moved back to her native village, West Grange, where Muncle and Mantie still lived, and looked for somewhere to live. She very much wanted children, not wanting to be left on her own considering the dangers he was facing, and so a year later I was born. He was on leave at that time, so he was on hand at the start of my life. They had digs in a big house in the village. After he went away to war again Mother found a little rented cottage in the village. "Six bob a week it was," she told me.

This is the first house I remember. It consisted of a living room, scullery and bedroom. There was no electricity, and water was heated on a big black range. There was an outside plumbed lavatory we shared with the Calders next door, along with a washhouse and coal sheds.

During embarkation leave the following year, my little brother Roly was conceived and my mother was very happy about it. Father was not on hand this time and in fact it was nearly two years before he and Roly met. He came home for good near the end of 1945.

I do remember some of the time before that. Roly was such a funny boy, he made us laugh all the time, except when he had his hair brushed. He had a huge mop of curly red hair, always tangled, and it hurt to brush and comb it. He had some teething problems and used to bite whatever came near him. I remember he took a piece out of a glass tumbler one time, and Mother had to fish it out of his mouth in a panic.

We had happy times. Every night at bedtime we said our prayers for Daddy to come home safe. Roly was full of fun and mischief then.

Then Father came home, and everything changed.

The first shadows

I remember he brought me a Greek soldier doll in a wooden box. They took the box away, as things like that were precious in the midst of wartime shortages, and I was not pleased. We kept the shoe cleaning stuff in it for ever after. I don't remember that he brought anything for Roly.

And Roly went quiet.

Long, long after, my mother told me what happened on Father's arrival. He had walked in and looked in horror at the cottage.

"Was this the best you could do?" he asked.

"Actually, yes," she replied, not understanding why he was asking.

"I can't live here," he went on cruelly. "I'm going home. And I'm taking Jeanie with me." Meaning me.

For once she stood up to him and refused to let me go. He went home to his parents' croft and stayed for several weeks. But of course it couldn't last. He needed his teaching job back, so back he came. He thought it a hovel, but it was home to us and we had been happy.

We children had been told he was coming home, and Roly, always excitable, was running about making us laugh as usual when Father arrived. Roly ran to him and clutched his leg, burying his face in his army trousers. I had a horrible feeling, and sure enough, he bit the trousers and nipped the leg underneath. Worse was to come.

Father picked him up and shook him like a rat. "Don't you ever do that again!" he roared at the poor child, who had no idea what he had done wrong.

From then on, Roly could do nothing right. He became quieter and quieter with each beating, until we hardly knew him. I too had my share of blame, but the savagery of Roly's treatment was very hard to bear. Roly resented this intrusion into our happy lives, and Father resented another male in the house, I think.

I do not now remember any particular incident in that house, though there were many. What I do remember is Auntie Bea, who was so good to us all. She knew, I think, what was happening, and could see the change in us. She would come down of an evening, sometimes with a parcel of chips inside her coat, and Father was always subdued when she was there. Looking back, I think she was one of the few people he had respect for, and she made him feel ashamed. She did not like him.

I craved the ability to read, so eventually, when I was four, my mother gave in and taught me. I took refuge (and have done ever since) in books. I would read to Roly sometimes, hoping to keep him quiet and unobserved. Then I went to school and one year later we reached the top of the housing list and moved a couple of miles away to a brand new house.

A bathroom! Electric lights! Such luxury. Indeed it was a nice house with a fairly big garden, and I thought this would please him.

Spiders and turnips

Roly and I shared a bedroom, which of course we were well used to. At the time I was six, Roly four. We were always sent to bed early, before we were properly tired, so of course we talked to one another for a while. Father would shout up "Be quiet, you two!" but only twice. After that, if we still talked, even whispered, up he came with the slipper and we had a good hiding. This was a weekly occurrence. The soundproofing was non-existent, and we could hear the children next door still playing long after we were in bed.

It was here that our mutual fear of spiders began. We had a washhouse and coal shed beside the back door. Big spiders roamed the washhouse, so we seldom went in there. Sometimes there would be one in our bedroom and we would ask Father to take it away. He did, but only after thrusting it at us both, scaring the daylights out of us. Even now, after various treatments, I cannot cope with big spiders.

There was also the ongoing verbal sarcasm and belittling. He never called Roly by his name, that I remember, although in fact it was a shortened version of his own name, Roderick. He called him "man". "Get a move on, man." "Sit still, man." "Eat your dinner, man." And so on.

I was luckily not a fussy eater, but I did not like the big yellow turnips he grew. Mother's soups were full of them and I wanted to leave them on the plate. No way would he let me. "I grow them, you eat them," he would say and stand over me till I managed to get them down. I couldn't even mash them into the soup, so he made me eat them in lumps.

Roly, however, had always been a picky eater. Small in frame, he didn't seem to need much in the way of nourishment. Particularly he did not like the fatty bits of meat. But he was never allowed to leave the table until his plate was empty. Goaded by remarks like "Be a man, not a baby, empty your plate," he would cry sometimes and be soundly smacked for it. I myself did not care for the fat, but I pretended it was peaches and managed to swallow it somehow. I knew what I would get if I left it. I tried to get Roly to do the same, but his imagination would not stretch to peaches. "It's greasy horrible," he would say, "it makes me feel sick."

I think we all knew what would happen if he *was* sick, so he kept it down.

At this point I must explain a peculiar thing. Although he was such a frightening bully to us in the home, if we were out among people, or if we had visitors, Father would be charm itself. He also treated us well in front of others, which I found very uncomfortable. And now and again he would sing to us. His father and brothers were all singers and he knew a lot of songs we had not heard of. So it was not all punishment. But you could never tell if it was going to be Jekyll or Hyde.

"You're a dirty brat"

The most damaging element in his cruelty was his sneering putdowns of us both. "You'll never amount to anything, you two, nobody will ever want to hear anything you say," was a common one. Worse than that, if we made a mess or didn't put toys away, was "You're a dirty filthy lazy brat." That was often.

I was always a wanderer. Gradually I began to know when he was spoiling for a spot of baiting or a beating; there was just something about his eyes and the way he looked at me. So if it was daylight I would go out with local children, or by myself, and wander the nearby field and burn till I thought the danger was over. If it was dark, of course, I just tried to be invisible.

I could never persuade Roly away from the house. He had a little friend next door and they played in our garden or his, so he was handy for a tongue lashing or a clout when the mood was on him. George was quite an open, outspoken child and of course Roly imitated him. Any words we were not allowed to say were soundly punished. 'Bum', I remember, was one of them. We were the children of a teacher, and were obliged to speak properly. Sex was a filthy, sinful thing, so we never mentioned our private parts out loud. Once in the bath I asked my mother what my nipples were for. She actually looked round to see if he could hear, then told me. "But we don't talk about them," she insisted.

CHAPTER TWO

Not long after we moved to our "luxury" new house, there was an outbreak of measles locally. Since we all played together, virtually all the children who had not already had measles fell victims. I had had the illness three years previously, aged three, but poor little Roly took it very badly.

The house we lived in had a "parlour" downstairs, in our case hardly ever used as such. We had a bed in there for visiting relatives, although now I do not ever remember having anybody staying.

Roly's brush with death

Roly collapsed at the tea table one evening. Father made

to grab him and make him eat whatever he was refusing, his usual tactic. For once Mum stepped in and pushed him away.

"Just look at this rash!" she said in horror. Roly was covered in a bright red rash, scary to see, and was foaming at the mouth and almost unconscious. Someone must have sent for the doctor, and he came quickly. By then Roly was laid out on the spare bed and Mum was sponging him down with cool water. He was talking, but not making sense.

There was a fairly big hallway where we often played and I hung about trying to hear what was being said. Frightening things. "Can't move him... keep him as cool as possible... will be back in the morning," From the doctor. Then, most scary of all: "if he lasts the night there's a chance."

I said my prayers that night with all the strength I had. Next morning there was no change; mother had been up all night trying to keep Roly's fever down. Auntie Bea appeared. We all loved her dearly, except Father. She banned us all from the bedroom where Mother was on constant duty, and tried to cheer me up and keep me busy. When I asked questions she just said "We have to hope the fever will break and there will be no damage." Damage? She wouldn't say what she meant by that.

It seemed at the time to go on for a long, long while, but looking back I expect it was only three or four days. I was allowed in at one point and Roly's poor, skinny body covered in spots made me cry, so I was banned again. The doctor came every day. Auntie Bea made meals and washed and ironed and helped Mum as much as she could. She came every morning early and stayed all day.

Finally came a terrible day. Roly screamed and screamed. The doctor said there was damage to his ear, and I heard "if it bursts outwards it might be all right, if it goes in we've lost him."

By then I couldn't eat or settle to anything. Already growing in me was BLAME. *This is due to all the beatings he has had from you*, I silently said to my father. *I hope this is a lesson*. Vain hope. I had seen him hitting Roly about the head and I was convinced he had caused something to go wrong.

I was given an aspirin that night (on a teaspoon of jam) and must have slept. In the morning all was quiet. With dread in my heart I crept downstairs. Auntie Bea was in the kitchen, *smiling*.

"You can go in, my love. He's better," she said.

I tiptoed in. They were both asleep and Roly looked cool. He was on his side with a towel under his head. I left before my knees gave way and burst into tears.

"There," Auntie said, "he will be better now. The doctor has been here most of the night. Roly's ear will leak for a while but he will recover. Breakfast for us now, I think?"

Well, Roly's ear did leak for a while and he was left with a slight deafness on that side and some recurring pain, but he did get better. My memory doesn't recall if the beatings stopped for any length of time, but if they did it was only a temporary lull.

Roly goes to school

Not very long after the measles, Roly was to start school. Now a strange thing happened, or at least it was strange to me.

My friends and I got the bus every morning into the village to attend the primary section of the local High School, where Father taught. But Roly was to go in the opposite direction to a different primary school. Of course I see now why Mum insisted on this, but at the time it seemed odd.

He loved it from the start, and was full of stories about the other children and the teachers. Things seemed better for a while, but Father had lost a certain amount of control and he did not like it. The verbal abuse was worse than ever, undermining Roly's new-found confidence. His school books were ridiculed and the school belittled.

Roly had made friends with a little girl who lived in a biggish house locally. She came with her mother to play one day and Father became the ideal parent, making them laugh and giving them things to do. I don't remember them ever coming back or Roly being invited to their house. The difference in Father when others were there was astonishing. Once or twice one or other of his brothers would come to stay and Father's voice changed back to his northern Scottish accent.

Speaking of his brothers, they all except one had children, roughly our age, with whom we got on well. None of the fathers ill-treated their children as he did, I am sure of that. He was the different one. In all my life, I cannot count the number of times someone has said to me "What a charming man your father is!" All I could ever answer was "Yes."

It was around this time that I began to notice how he treated my mother. She was clearly afraid of him, and deferred to him on every decision. He was very much in charge and she seldom argued with him. She was good at practical things and he was not. I remember the old wireless set would go crackly at times. She would put it on the table, strip out all its valves, then give them a dust and put them back in the right place. He was always out or busy when this happened. If plugs had to be changed, she did it. He did no housework, but called us dirty and lazy if we did not help out.

Worms

Barely a year after Roly had been so ill with measles, there was an outbreak of worms amongst the local children.

The treatment at that time was a large dose of Epsom salts followed by a whole day of no solid food – it may have been the other way round. I only remember the worst part of it. I was seven and Roly five, and our mother had diagnosed worms in both of us.

We were warned in advance of the treatment, so I at least was prepared for an uncomfortable 24 hours. When I got up in the morning, mother was waiting with half a tumbler of milky liquid for me. Roly trotted into the kitchen after me, and as the elder I had the privilege of going first. We knew it would not taste nice, so I knocked it back in short order. It was very bitter and I made a face.

That was enough for poor Roly, who refused to drink his dose. I was appalled. I just knew what would happen now, and deeply regretted making a face. I tried to say it really didn't taste all that bad, but Roly wouldn't budge. To this day I blame myself for making a face.

It being Saturday, Father was still in bed while all this was going on. Voices were raised, with all three of us involved, and they woke the sleeping dragon. Downstairs he came, brandishing a book. It was a red covered hardback I remember.

"What's going on?" he was furious.

Mother explained that Roly was refusing to drink his half-tumbler of salts.

"Right," said he, "double the quantity."

I was horrified. Roly shaking and terrified, still with his mouth tightly shut. Mother produced a whole tumblerful.

BAM went the book on Roly's backside. He still wouldn't drink. BAM BAM went the book on whatever part of Roly he could reach. He held the child with one hand and went on hitting him with the book, it seemed like forever. Roly went limp eventually, glazed about the eyes, and drank the whole dose of salts. He then collapsed on the floor, while I was in floods of tears and trying to be invisible. I paid no attention to my mother, who must have been upset; I was blaming myself too much for

Roly's possible death. I really thought he had killed him this time.

I remember no more about the rest of the treatment. Presumably it worked, as the worms disappeared and Roly recovered.

I relive the whole incident often, still full of blame and regret.

CHAPTER THREE

One day not long after my seventh birthday I came home from school to a big surprise. We had been given a piano! There was a piano in the parlour at Muncle and Mantie's house, but we were never allowed to touch it, not that either of us at that age wanted to. Now we had one of our own and I was to have music lessons every Saturday morning.

I cannot now remember if I was pleased about this at the time; all I know is that it very soon bored me to tears. What a waste of a Saturday morning. It was clear to me from the start that I had no talent for the piano, or indeed any interest in playing. But both parents had wanted to learn and been denied, so I had to keep trying. I was made to practise, even on sunny summer evenings when I could hear other children still outside.

This went on and on and on, until at age 14 I defied them both and refused to have any more fruitless lessons. I was punished, of course, but I stuck to my guns and hardly ever touched a piano thereafter.

Roly had displayed an unexpected talent, however, and played far better than I did, although he refused to read music. He played by ear, so he was excused piano lessons long before I was.

Shillings and postal orders

For birthdays and Christmas we were sent postal orders by well-meaning aunts. An elderly uncle would give us £1 each for birthday and at Christmas. For these we were made to write thank-you letters, but the money was taken from us and we never saw it again. I used to hope they would give me an actual present, maybe a book, but they never did.

It seemed to me unfair, but I assumed this happened in every family. Gradually I realised that this was not the case. Other children were allowed to spend their birthday money on going to the pictures, or sweets or some book or toy. We were not given any pocket money until we went to secondary school, and then it was such a small amount it bought a packet of fruit gums maybe twice a week. As a perpetually hungry child this seemed not nearly enough. Though not what I would consider well off, we were certainly not poor, so I still don't understand the logic behind this deprivation.

One incident replays in my mind to this day. We were to go on a visit to Granny, my mother's mother. This entailed two longish bus journeys to get there, so we did not visit her often. I wore my school blazer for the occasion. I was eight years old, Roly six.

It was a lovely visit. Granny's house was very old and full of mysterious rooms, and there was a large, dark washhouse outside which we liked to explore. Years later I learned that the house was full of dry rot, which accounted for the weird smell everywhere, but for a child it was an exciting place.

Before we left, Granny gave us each a shilling. I was allowed to receive it, of course, but knew it would have to be surrendered when we got home. I put it in the breast pocket of my blazer. When we got home it was very late and we were put immediately to bed.

Next day was a school day, and none of us

remembered the shillings. I left my blazer as usual in the school cloakroom. When I got home, both parents were waiting for me. Father held out his hand. I knew immediately what he wanted and reached into my breast pocket. No shilling. My heart went cold. I knew what that meant.

We had been well warned at school not to leave valuables in our coats, but somehow I had forgotten what was in my blazer and I just knew that it would be my fault and I was in for severe punishment. The look in his icy eyes was enough.

I stammered that the money wasn't there and he roared into my face, "I knew it. You've spent it on rubbish, haven't you? HAVEN'T YOU?"

I knew from experience that the easiest thing was to admit the sin I was being accused of, but this seemed so unfair that I said "No, I haven't. Someone must have taken it from my jacket in the cloak...."

I didn't get to finish before the first blow fell. He hit me hard on the head and I fell over. He kept repeating, "You spent it, admit it or hand it over."

In the end of course I had to say that I had indeed spent it, and was given a long session of verbal abuse and the slipper on the backside.

Some weeks later, my mother asked me if I had anything to be mended. Sunday evening in those days was mending time, socks to be darned, holes to be mended, buttons sewn back on.

I had noticed that the school badge on my blazer was beginning to come off. The stitching had given way along the top.

As she took it from me, a shilling piece fell out from between the badge and the pocket. Father was there and I couldn't stop myself blurting out "the shilling Granny gave me!"

So stupid of me, and I instantly regretted it. He grabbed me by the shoulders and shook me like a rat. "Don't you EVER look at me like that again!" he shouted. If he couldn't get you on a real sin, it was the way you looked at him. Many and many a time I have suffered from "looking at him that way."

So that time I had two hidings for doing absolutely nothing.

And he took the shilling.

It wasn't until I was about 14 years old that I challenged my mother to let me keep any money that was given to me as a present. I don't know what she said to him, but after that I was allowed to spend it on something useful, as long as it was suitable. A dynamo for my bike was one that lasted a long time.

Other bullies

During my four years at West Grange school, before we moved to Bellwick, I had a variety of teachers, all women. Most were good teachers, some were likeable, some were cold, and a few were either sadistic or mad.

If you were good at your lessons, they mostly left you alone. The instrument of punishment was the tawse. My father had two of these, and they sat curled up on his desk for us all to see. The tawse was a strip of thick leather, divided into two half way along its length. Some of my teachers would smack you with their hand only, while some used the tawse, and I tell you it was sore. I well remember having my knuckles rapped with a ruler often for not paying attention.

We had one teacher who never gave out punishment of any kind. The result was that nobody paid much attention in her lessons and the disruptive pupils ruled. So that was no use.

Most dealt fairly with us all, and most of us had our

share of punishments. One, however, was worse than all the rest put together. I will call her Miss G. She taught what is now Primary 4, so we were all about eight or nine. None of us liked her. Strangely, during her time with us she got married. We were all amazed. Who would be daft enough to marry her, we thought? She became Mrs B.

Because she knew my father, who taught the "Qually", what is now Primary 7, she gave me special treatment, praising me unduly. I found this extremely embarrassing and uncomfortable. Those children who found it difficult to keep up she thrashed unmercifully. She just loved to make us cry.

One of the boys, Wally, never cried. She saw this as a challenge and never let up on him. She would belt him and shake him but he just went white and said nothing. One terrible day she was in a foul mood. She picked Wally up by the shoulders and shook him and slapped him until some of us thought we should go for help. By a miracle, the classroom door opened behind her back and the headmaster stood and watched, only for a few seconds.

"Mrs B," he said, not loudly, but loud enough. She dropped poor Wally like a hot potato and went beetroot red. The headmaster pointed a finger in the direction of his room, and walked out. She followed. We waited in silence. She did not return. Another teacher came and finished the lesson.

I do not now remember if she ever came back. Years later I told my mother about the incident, and she remembered hearing about it at the time. "The woman should never have been allowed to teach," she said. "We all knew she was mad."

There were plenty of bullies among the pupils, but because they knew my father was a teacher I was spared most of their attentions. The one I suffered most from for all of my childhood, apart from Father, was my mother's adopted sister Kate. Luckily, while we were at West Grange we saw very little of her.

My Granny Lizzie and her husband Bill, whom I always called Grampa, had two children from their marriage, Margaret and George. When George was about 13 or so, they adopted a young child from a children's home. I have no idea why they did this, as they were far from well off. Maybe it was to make up for having my mother taken care of by others; I can only guess.

Kate was always horrible to me. Six years older, she bullied me from the start. If she could get me into trouble, she would, though I needed no help from her. Her favourite party piece was to make me giggle at the table, for she knew I would be punished for it. I was a terrible giggler, and so was Roly, and she knew how to do it.

Sometimes when we were older, she would try to get me to attract the attention of the local farmers' sons. I would refuse and her answer was always the same. : "Do it or I will tell your mother you did such and such." That was always something bad.

"But I never did," I would protest.

"I know that, but I'm older than you and she will believe me."

I couldn't be sure she was right, but sometimes I did what she wanted to keep her quiet.

She was a stupid girl who did nothing at school, and resented me for being the opposite. She would tell tales, mostly untrue, and I would be for it again. Mercifully she mostly left Roly alone.

She went too far one evening when she spotted me doing homework and asked about it. It happened to be Latin and she sneered and sniggered and told me that would never put a penny in my pocket. Father overheard her and gave her a prizewinning tongue-lashing, much to my glee.

The Library

Also when I was seven, I asked if I could join the local library. Most of my classmates had joined and I envied them the choice of children's books in our library. I cannot understand why I was not allowed to join. I always looked after books and devoured any that came my way. I would have been far happier in there on a Saturday morning than pounding away on the boring old piano and getting nowhere. But because they had been denied the tuition they wanted, I had to have it even if I didn't want it. So unfair.

This was one of the times when my fear of Father came second to my desire to read new things. I approached Mum first, and she said no, but gave no reason. I then very bravely asked Father, and he snapped that I had already been told, so they had obviously discussed it.

It may seem a trivial thing to deny me library membership, but both parents knew how much I enjoyed books, and I believed then and still believe now it was deliberate cruelty to do what they did.

I went into the library on my way home from school one day, became immersed in a book and was late home.

I confessed where I had been and was soundly thrashed for "dishonesty."

It occurred to me long after that this was part of the severe censorship imposed on us in all directions. We were allowed comics, we had the *Beano* and the *Dandy* between us, then the *Eagle* appeared, which was apparently acceptable, and I had the *Girls' Crystal*, because there were no picture stories in it, only narrative, so that was edifying.

There were programmes on the wireless that we would have enjoyed, and other school friends discussed them endlessly, but because they were in broad Scots or slightly suggestive, they were thought to be a bad example for us and were banned. Any books we read at home were examined before we were allowed to read them.

I remember a summer day in the garden next door discussing a story we had had at school. It was about a genie who had granted three wishes. There were four or five of us seven or eight-year-old girls. One girl said "If you had three wishes, what would they be?"

I forget what they all wished for, mostly it was lots of money and toys etc. My turn came, and I was in no doubt; first, I would like to be a bird and be able to fly anywhere. Second, I would like to join the library. Third, I would like to be grown up. How they laughed!

How much do my three wishes tell about my seven-year-old self? All I wanted was freedom. I think it was about then that I realised I was different, and I didn't like to be.

CHAPTER FOUR

We stayed in that house for three years. Life carried on as before, with verbal abuse daily, and physical abuse always a probability for both of us.

Because my mother had taught me to read before I went to school, I had missed out the first class, with the result that I was always a year younger than the class average. Counting and writing were a struggle to begin with, but eventually I caught up with my classmates and began to do quite well in school. In a class of 30 or so, I regularly came fourth or fifth. Never once did I receive any praise or encouragement from either parent, but I tried so hard, I see now, just to prove him wrong. He said I would never amount to anything, and I thought stubbornly that he might be mistaken.

Roly's school results were ridiculed, no matter how good they were considering his serious illness before he started school. Father would lock the bathroom door with him and Roly inside and I would disappear outside before the screams started. Why didn't she do something? I will never know. I considered myself lucky that my results got no reaction at all.

I became aware that there was something happening. Whispering and discussing and stuff made me nervous, especially when I couldn't hear what it was about. I was a particularly inquisitive child, maybe because I was watching for the temper signs. "What have I done now?" I thought.

On the move

One day when we were having tea with Auntie Bea, they told us. Father had been promoted and been given a small rural school on the other side of the county. He would be headmaster, with four classes, and there was another teacher who had the first three classes. We would be moving during the Easter holidays.

We were struck dumb. As I remember it, Roly cried. He did not like change. I asked as many questions as I was allowed. Neither parent had seen the school or the house we would be living in, so they couldn't give me much information.

It began to sound quite exciting, very open countryside, and to cheer Roly up I pretended to be pleased about it. Alas, this upset Auntie Bea, who said "Are you so anxious to leave us all?" I hadn't thought of that, and of course we would never have chosen to leave her, but it was too late.

Actually I was rather pleased, as unlike Roly I liked change, and felt it was sometimes not a bad thing. Maybe with a new and more responsible job, Father would be better tempered.

At last the day came. Father went with the furniture van, but there was no room for all of us, so we had to take two long bus journeys and then walk a mile to our new home.

Bellwick

I will never forget our first sight of Bellwick. We turned a corner at the top of a hill, and there it was spread out before us. We had been told there was a castle, but this was nothing like any castle I had seen in books. In reddish stone, it was a tall building with very narrow windows and a wide ledge on the roof. It was surrounded by a high wall with a circular gatehouse at the entrance. It delighted my romantic mind. Other than that there was a church at the castle gate, and hidden in trees a large manse. In front of the manse was a lovely little house with a long garden, ending in the school playground.

The romance was knocked out of me when we saw the inside of the house, however. Again there was no electricity, and as this was April it was very cold. Another big black range stood in the kitchen and there was a gas ring in the long bleak scullery. But there were seven rooms!

There were a couple of farms very near, with their attendant cottages, so it was not all that isolated. And the village was only a mile away. I thought it paradise, and looked forward to a big explore.

Nothing much changed in our relationship with our parents. Punishments were still regular, and if we had done nothing to deserve it, Father made something up. "Don't speak back to me, ever." Or "How dare you look at me like that!" There was always something. And the slippers were now abandoned in favour of a leather belt. He would look at me and slowly take off that belt, and as he did so, he would whistle gently under his breath. To this day, when I hear someone whistling like that, my blood runs cold.

A year later, two momentous things happened. The first was that electricity came to Bellwick. There were months of work for the electrical workers, putting up poles, cutting back trees, etc. We had great fun watching them, though we had been warned not to get in their way. Of course it was fine to have lights you could put on with a switch, but I missed the familiar hiss of the oil lamps and the heat they gave off.

A new puppy

The other momentous happening was that we got a dog. Mother came home from Edinburgh one day with a little orange bundle inside her coat. She had been to a pet shop where there was a litter of mongrel puppies for sale. All were black except one, which was ginger, so she took it. We called her Lady.

How that poor dog suffered! Father was so hard on her and she was only a few weeks old. She was house trained very quickly, for she knew she would be whipped if she made a mess.

Roly, who was afraid of his own shadow at that time, was scared to death of this little pup, for a time at least. Strangely enough, she was always Father's dog, for all that he hit her so often. She followed him everywhere. She grew into a very independent and strong-minded animal, and we loved her dearly.

Around this time Roly was to move up to the "big" room at school. This meant he would be taught by Father, and I know Roly was dreading it. It was obvious to the whole classroom that the poor boy could do nothing right. Time after time he was sent out to the staff room to await another belting. I tried to see what he was doing wrong, but there was nothing. At the same time, I had to be careful, for everything I did was noticed and I got many a tongue-lashing for quite understandable mistakes. He had to make us look small, it seemed.

One of my good friends, Ronald, asked me one day why the "Maister" was so hard on Roly. "You tell me," I replied. All the locals called him the Maister, and I think he liked it.

But Roly survived four years of his father's teaching and beatings.

High School

At the age of 11, it was time for me to go to the local High School. This meant leaving home at 7.30 am and being back just before 5 pm. As a very active, sporty child, and faced with a long journey to and from school, I was always hungry.

Centred on the castle, Bellwick was very much a rural community. The castle has an interesting history. Mary Queen of Scots is supposed to have escaped from there dressed as a page. They say Cromwell fired cannon at the back of it. Certainly there is a large area of damage there, but with walls twelve feet thick he did not make much impression.

The 200 yards of driveway end in iron gates, next to the churchyard, and the church also has a long history. I remember it as a freezing cold place which smelled musty.

The Schoolhouse stood almost at these gates, where a little road led round to the manse. Schoolmasters and ministers must have been expected to have large families once, for the manse had twelve rooms and the schoolhouse seven. Both gardens were huge, each with a tumbledown pigsty, great for exploring.

At the end of the schoolhouse garden was the school

playground. The school had three large classrooms, a staff room, lavatory and broom cupboard, as well as two cloakrooms for our outdoor stuff. Each classroom had a big fireplace, all used in winter as the school was so cold. We also had a fire on the coldest days in the Playshed, a unique building in the playground.

The younger children had the first classroom and the older ones the third. The middle room was used as storage and also for the boys' handwork sessions.

I have said nothing about Father's teaching abilities. In fact he was a very good teacher, if on the strict side. He seemed to be able to control his temper better in school than at home. His favourite topic was nature, and we learned a great deal from him on the subject.

In addition to him, we had four "travelling" teachers every week, one for the girls' handwork, one for art, one for music, and the last for PT, Physical Training as it was called then. Father took the boys for handwork, although what he taught them I cannot imagine, as other than gardening, he had no interest in or ability to do crafts.

On the other side of the school from the schoolhouse stood the Hall. This was a long wooden building, home for dozens of rats, where every local function took place. We also used it for school dinners, PT, and Christmas parties. The Women's Rural Institute, always called the Rural, met there. There were whist drives, dances (music provided by the local accordionist), sales of work and so on. I myself never saw a rat there, but we were all aware of the possibility. After the dances, which of course we were not allowed to attend, all kinds of interesting things were to be found at the back of the hall – buttons, coins sometimes, once a pair of knickers.

That was the centre of Bellwick. Other than that there were a few farms with their attendant cottages, and a couple of large houses belonging to the castle estate and rented out.

Most of the school pupils belonged to Midwick, a village which was nearly a mile away and on a bus route. The rest were farmers' or farm workers' children. There was a lot of poverty, I remember, and shoes were patched with cardboard and such.

Some of the pupils would ask me what it was like to be taught by my father. Knowing nothing else, what could I say? I called him 'Sir' in the school just as the rest did. In a way he was two different people in my life, and at work by far the easier.

At that time there was a (to my eyes very old) lady who cleaned the school and the hall and dished up the school dinners. In fact she did more than that; she was midwife and layer out, and she "did" for the manse. The school at that time had girls' and boys' lavatories outside in the playground, and she cleaned them every day. They regularly froze in winter, of course, and she dealt with that too. The smell of Jeyes fluid still reminds me of those outside lavvies. She always called him "Maister" and he enjoyed that.

It was there, inevitably, that we learned about sex. It was a taboo subject at home, and I listened avidly to the lurid tales from those children who had older siblings and who "knew it all." Were it not for those children, I would have entered my teens knowing nothing at all. As it was, I grew up believing it to be dirty and furtive and not to be spoken about in company.

More censorship

After we moved to Bellwick, to the countryside I came to love, I became aware of just how much I was controlled. I do realise that parents have an obligation to protect their children from bad people.

We lived in the Schoolhouse, right next to the school. During the summer holidays, groups were allowed to camp out in the school for a week at a time. This was very interesting for us, for we could not be prevented from seeing these children and in fact joining in with them.

The Hall was also used by visiting groups. A Jewish organisation came every summer for a day and had a huge picnic, in the Hall if it was raining, in a neighbouring field if it was fair. Didn't we look forward to that! They brought an ice cream machine and a vanload of goodies, which we were invited to share. They were such nice people, and I wish I could thank them now for the temporary pleasure they gave to Roly and me. Alas, I overdid the ice cream one year and had a bout of colic all night. But it was well worth it.

The first group to stay in the school came when I was about 11. They were cub scouts from Edinburgh, along with their leaders. Every evening they had a camp fire in the field behind the school and wonder of wonders, we were allowed to be there. This was a sing song, and we fried sausages over the fire, something entirely new for Roly and me, which we enjoyed very much. The cub leaders were very respectable ladies, so I guess that's why we were allowed. Of course, they thought the world of "The Maister."

I made friends with one young cub and after they left

he wrote me a letter, saying how much he had enjoyed his week and hoped that he would one day come back to Bellwick. I did not expect the letter, and it was handed to me, opened, with the advice, "Do not answer this."

Before I could stop myself, I cried, "Why?"

"Because I say so," was the reply.

I then realised that every letter I had ever received had already been opened. At age 11, I could not see why I wasn't allowed privacy, and I still can't.

The following year, a group of Baptists came to camp in the school. They were all girls, so I was allowed to go among them. I even spent one night sleeping on a straw mattress with them. They were all slightly older than I was, and there was talk of boyfriends and things I knew very little about. I made friends with one girl, Annie, and she made me laugh. After they had gone, she wrote to me, as the cub had done, thanking me for being friends and hoping we might meet again one day. She had added an extra page with a joke on it. I do not remember the joke, it couldn't have been explicit or I would not have understood it, but it was funny. It so happened that I met the postman at the gate that day, and was able to read my letter before they got it. I stuffed the extra page in my knickers and handed over the letter as usual.

He knew. I do not know how, but he did. I was forbidden to write to Annie, but for once I disobeyed. I asked her not to refer to my letters but just to be chatty, but there were no more letters from her. I suspect she sent some, but they did not reach me.

Another censorship disobedience got me into trouble. One of the children in the country school had an older brother in the army. This brother used to send American horror comics, which were shared among us all, and well worn by the time we had had our turn. The Maister knew about them and told me not to read them. How could I not? They were very scary, which I loved, but one night I had a terrible nightmare and screamed out. I screamed a lot more when he hit me for reading "trash."

It was better when I went to the High School, for I could join the library, which was next door, and share comics with other girls. I seemed to spend much of my time concealing library cards and books or pretending that they were part of our English course.

Father's secret

On the same subject, my mother had a half-brother still at home with his mother Lizzie, who seemed to have a supply of magazines which were "not for our eyes". I used to watch them changing hands with Father and wondered what they were and where they were kept. Granny's house was a lot more relaxed about reading materials, but I never found them there.

But I found them at home, an event which I will come to later.

I had made friends with a local farmer's son, Marty, who was the same age as me. We got on very well and roamed the countryside together, rain or shine. However, Marty had a happy home life with an older sister and brother and he had no idea how I was treated in my own home.

At the time I started at secondary school, so did he. Alas, he was sent to a school in Edinburgh, twice as far away as my local high school, and we began to grow apart, both making new friends.

He too had a long day, and shared my constant hunger. His remedy was simple. There was no shortage of food on the farm, so he just helped himself to extra in his schoolbag every day. Sometimes he would share with me on the bus going home, but usually there was none left by then. We were both active children, playing sports and seldom still; no wonder we were constantly hungry.

I become a thief

One day I told Marty about never having any money of my own, and he was horrified. He had generous relatives and was allowed to spend whatever they gave him.

"They have no right to keep your money," he said, outraged. "Why don't you just take it back? Or keep it?"

I couldn't tell him what would happen to me if I did, but for a while I took his advice and helped myself to any odd change that I could find in pockets and drawers. With this I bought food. Of course, eventually I was caught. I think now that I always knew I would be caught, and hoped it would bring things to a head.

This happened when I was 13, when the years of fear and hurt became mixed up with a bad adolescence, periods, lack of confidence and so on. My school work suffered, because I knew there was no point in trying to do well, nobody seemed to care. I went through about six months of doing what I pleased, knowing I would be punished for nothing anyway. I wasn't too fussy about washing myself or wearing clean clothes.

This made such a bad atmosphere in the house that I seriously thought of running away or killing myself. I could only have run to Auntie Bea, who would have brought me straight back, so that was a non-starter.

I do not now remember just how I was caught, but I do recall it was a Friday, because we had been to music lessons. As soon as I walked in I knew. He stood there waiting, his eyes glittering like icicles. I quailed.

He pointed at Roly first. "You! Upstairs, now."

A strange thing happened then. Mother stepped in between us and said "I will deal with this." And he backed away!

She took me into the front room, which was seldom used. I confessed as soon as she accused me, and she asked me why I had done it. I explained about the postal orders and about always being hungry.

"Ah," she said, "I thought so."

She told me then that she had saved all the money we had been given in National Savings certificates "for a time when you might need it." And I remembered taking money to school every week when we were still at West Grange and having savings stamps to take home.

"Why didn't you tell me all this?" I was curious.

"I thought you would know, " she answered. "I see now that I should have."

"He's going to punish me," I said, resigned, thinking well at least I knew what I was being punished for, and it was something real. I deserved it.

"Not this time," she replied. "now this is what I suggest."

She went on to tell me I would be given extra food to take to school, and also extra pocket money. But she would expect some changes from me also. She had noticed my scruffy appearance and that I didn't put much in the way of clothes in the wash. I agreed that my behaviour would change, and she left it at that.

I do not know how she overruled him that one time, but I should have known that he would not leave it at that. The next day he trapped me in the scullery and let me have it.

I was standing beside a mirror. I could see most of my face in the mirror. I dared not look at him, so I watched the girl in the mirror, imagining it to be someone who was not me. As he lashed out horrible things at me, this girl's face got whiter and whiter and huge tears rolled down her face. I was not aware of crying, for I knew that was what he wanted, but without moving a muscle these big tears splashed down on the floor. I can see her now.

I don't remember one word of what he said, but character assassination is putting it mildly. No one would ever, ever want anything to do with a filthy, lying thief like me. I would never amount to anything and he was bitterly ashamed to be my father. I suffered torture that day, worse than I could have imagined. Believing I deserved every word made it even more unbearable.

I think that was the day I started building a wall round myself, so that he could never reach me. Years later, actually just after he died, I had counselling, for his death did not bring the relief I always imagined it would. I told this story to the counsellor. She advised me to contact the child I had been then, if I could, and give her comfort, tell her that he was wrong. I thought it good advice, but when I tried, the wall was there still, and I couldn't get through. How odd.

Appendicitis

Soon after that horrible experience I was taken ill with appendicitis, at only just 14. Everything seemed to change at that time. While I was away from home for the two-week recovery time I was able to see how wrong I had been. And also how wrong my father had been. I was able to talk to my mother when I got home, to tell her how I felt and how I had hoped to die. Physically that was my release from pain. He never beat me again, though the verbal abuse continued.

Actually there was just one more incident that I clearly remember. It happened just before the appendicitis. He was in great demand locally as a member of various committees, and also to give references and so on. One day not long after my operation, we were told a lady would be coming to see him and he would want tea brought in. My mother and I had had a disagreement and I was unhappy about helping her with this. Anyway, I took in teacups and plates of scones at the required time, and this lady said "There's a good girl, helping your mummy".

For some reason I glanced at him, and the ice in his eyes was fair warning. I just knew I was for it. The lady left and he marched me up to my room. Then he laid about me with his belt, saying all the while, "You know what this is for". I did not know what it was for, but if I had said "no", I thought he would have carried on till he killed me, so I said "yes".

To this day I have no idea who the lady was, or what I had done wrong. I suspect the interview was some kind of criticism or complaint, which would not have pleased him, so he took it out on me, as was his way. Roly, wisely, was nowhere near on that day.

This foreknowledge of what was to come was something I had learned over the years. I seldom gave him eye contact, as his eyes when he was in a temper would freeze your blood. But I usually knew when trouble was coming, and if at all possible I would disappear till the danger was past. Roly couldn't or didn't know it was danger time, so he usually got the worst of it.

That, I think, was the last time he laid hands on me.

I had a difficult adolescence, not surprisingly. I worked hard at school after I realised it made no difference whether I did or not. I found I enjoyed learning.

I had agreed with my mother that we would be allowed to keep at least some of our birthday money and she would give me pocket money if I did housework when asked. So I began to go to the pictures on a Saturday in a crowd from school. There were boys in the group, but I lied to my father about that or I would have been called filthy names. I think he suspected. Till his dying day, if I told a lie to my father, it didn't count as a lie.

Around the same time, there was another incident I clearly remember. There had been a visitor, I forget who it was, and after he left I had no time to disappear, but I kept quiet and he grabbed poor Roly, picked him up screaming and kicking, carried him into the bathroom and locked the door. I gave my mother one unforgiving look and fled the house.

★ ★ ★

Not surprisingly, Roly also had a difficult adolescence. I was aware of this, and tried to help, for all the good it was.

Like me, he knew that it didn't matter how he behaved, the beatings would go on. And on. He became highly excitable, shouting and capering, probably because he knew he was for it anyway. Father called it "showing off", but I knew the poor lad could not help it.

Report card time was the worst. It did not seem to matter if we had done well or badly, it was never good enough. There were subjects we did not do so well at, and they were the ones he pounced on. As exam time approached, Roly got wilder and wilder in his behaviour. I remember waking up in the middle of a particular night, hearing a strange voice in Roly's room. This was the doctor, and my heart went cold. My first thought was to wonder if Father had killed Roly at last.

I listened at my door. The doctor decided it must be a "grumbling appendix" as he could find nothing definite.

Exams were to start the next day. I do not remember if these exams were any different, if the report cards were worse or better, but I do know that Roly was in genuine pain that night, real or imagined it made no difference, and he was made to go to school next morning. I still think it was fear. We lived most of our lives at that time in fear.

Our first car

Around this time, too, Father decided he would have a car. In the army, he had been driving various vehicles. His lesson had been, "This is a truck. This is the brake, here's where the fuel goes. Now drive it." There was no time for proper training. This meant that he did not have to take a driving test in civilian life; his army licence was enough.

So he acquired an old Wolseley and we were mobile. Heavens, but he was a bad driver. I only agreed to be a passenger reluctantly. But he was like a dog with two tails.

This meant something else to me. He and Mum would go out for "a run" most days after the evening meal, leaving me to clear up the dishes. For a blessed hour we had peace in the house. I could relax.

One day I was looking through the bookshelf for something to read. I was now tall enough to reach the top shelf, though of course there was nothing remotely unsuitable on display. Tucked in at the back were some lurid paperbacks I had not seen before, "master and slave" type novels. Wow, I thought, he's human. I put them back, but it made me wonder if there might be more stuff hidden somewhere that I wasn't meant to see.

Setting Roly to watch for the car coming back, I looked in his wardrobe. Sure enough, some magazines were there in a box away at the back. By modern standards these were no more than mildly suggestive, and most of the jokes I didn't quite understand, but the fact that he had hidden them gave me a good feeling. I was not allowed any privacy, but it made me feel somehow that I was a better person than he.

So I had a lot to thank the car for.

CHAPTER FIVE

———◆———

By now we were 16 and 14 and Roly at last was beginning to grow and fill out. He too had a friend, and this I believe had helped him through all the punishments and beatings. Our friends knew nothing of how we were treated, but I wonder if they suspected.

Where we lived was a local beauty spot, much frequented by visitors especially in the summer months, for the castle had an interesting history and the church had kept some medieval features. There would be cyclists, motorists, hikers, all sorts on a fine day.

Unwelcome visitors

The last truly unpleasant incident that I remember

happened on such a day. I was out in the garden, while Roly was cleaning his bike. I realised that two cyclists had stopped and were looking at the castle, and that they were two boys in my year at school. My heart went cold. I don't think they had seen me, though they probably knew I lived there, so I shot into the house and became busy in the kitchen. I prayed that Roly wouldn't see them.

My prayers were in vain. Father was also in the kitchen and Roly came running in, his face alight. I glared at him, as if to say "Don't say a word!" but out it came.

"Do you see who's out front?" he asked, and named them.

The wrath of God rose from his chair and made for me.

"Are they here sniffing round you?" he roared, "get up to your room, you filthy brat, and don't come out till I tell you."

Roly tried to back out. "They're only out for a run," he began, but too late. I went upstairs and shut myself in my room. Hours later I crept out when all was quiet. I felt dirty and despairing.

We had had friends to the house before, and as long as he knew they were coming all was well. I am at a loss to understand why he reacted in the way he did. I only know that I was quite sure he would. I usually knew how he would behave, what I never knew was why.

Father loses his grip

It was soon after that that Father began to lose his power over us. I have a photo of Roly and me on the day we both left school. We are the same height. We started work almost immediately and not long after that we moved house yet again. Father was to be headmaster of a much larger school nearer Edinburgh, so it was convenient for Roly and me to travel to work.

After six months or so, Roly decided to go to sea. I thought that was a wonderful idea, and off he went. I stayed at home still, although I could have moved out as well, and my mother took a temporary teaching job, so things were very different.

Without his control over all of us, Father had a mental breakdown and lost his job. We moved again while he recovered, which took a year or so, and he managed to get a minor teaching post eventually. I moved out and went to live in Edinburgh. Roly came home on leave, a different person. He had grown in height and width and in confidence, all credit to him. It was wonderful to see.

★ ★ ★

Once Father had lost the control which seemed to be so important to him, he became, at least for the most part, a different person. Or so it seemed.

I got married and had a son and a daughter. My parents seemed to be very fond of my children, but I was cautious about babysitting, remembering my own brutal childhood. No-one was going to ill-treat my children. Strangely, this never happened. Both children had much to do with both grandparents, and adored them. The Maister was teaching again in a rural school very similar to Bellwick, and they had plenty of room to spare, so my two spent many happy holidays with them. It seemed to me, once I felt more sure of their safety, that he was making up for his failings as a parent by being the best grandfather he could be. And he was.

I did notice that he still treated my mother much the same. I would take her out on her own sometimes and she would ramble on about the way he was with her. I had heard it all before, and was sorry for her. But he was fine with my children, so I was content.

As is natural, as my children grew older they grew

away from us and from their grandparents. I noticed that Father once more was restless as his power dwindled.

I recall only one unpleasant incident. My daughter, aged 16, was spending the weekend with them. On the Sunday she asked if she could go to church with them. It was summer, and she had borrowed a skirt from me, as she ran about in jeans mostly. This was a black broderie anglaise skirt with a black underskirt, quite respectable if not very smart. He took one look and told her he wasn't going with her looking indecent.

My poor daughter was so upset. She came home to me in distress and told me about it. For the first time in my 42 years I lifted the phone and raged at him. I quite forgot that I had never done such a thing ever before and really went to town on him. I couldn't stand up for myself, but I was like a tiger when my child was threatened. I had never heard him apologise in my whole life, and he did not then. I remember telling him that he would die a lonely old man. He didn't care.

CHAPTER SIX

All through my adult life, no matter how much I tried to forget, my abuse in childhood has affected me. I have never lost my terror of spiders, despite several different treatments. With a lot of hard work it has diminished, but it has never gone away.

I have missed a great deal of fun through being unsociable. Bearing in mind that "nobody would seek my company or want to hear anything I had to say", I have avoided parties and outings as much as I could. When forced to be in company I am mostly silent, and therefore accused of being "snooty". Public speaking was torture and interviews very difficult, though I failed very few of those. I had a deal of stubbornness which helped me there.

Having children helped me also. Determined not to

make the same mistakes my parents made, of course I made different ones, but there was no deliberate cruelty and no brutal beatings. I was subject to occasional spells of black depression, and at those times I relied heavily on my mother to help.

Perhaps the biggest difficulty I had was with sex. Having had it drummed into me that this was a horrible, filthy thing not to be spoken about, it took a long time and a great deal of patience before I realised that it was something to be enjoyed, and not to be ashamed of.

More new beginnings

My marriage ended, as so many do, when both children had left school and would not be too much affected. It was amicable but final.

In spite of Father telling me I would never amount to anything, I had stayed in a secure job and had several promotions, so I was well able to support myself. Slowly, gradually, I had proved him at least partially wrong. I had gone back to work some years before, and although I never liked the job much, I was good at it and moved steadily up the ladder.

By then I could spot bullying and potential bullying

immediately. It was difficult to avoid, and easy to monitor, though it made me sad. Our office had a Training Section, where employees new to the system started. They were then passed to the individual section where they were to work for what they called "desk training".

The Training Officer at the time was – let me say – indiscreet. He should not have discussed the new people with anybody while they were training, but he did, loud and long.

One day he brought Graham to our section and allocated one of his own friends to desk train the poor lad, another lady who was considerably less than tactful. We all already knew that Graham was struggling with the system, so I watched the whole proceedings with sympathy for him. He was a mild-mannered, quiet, friendly soul and I liked him.

Graham was what I considered a square peg in a round hole, having good educational qualifications but unable to grasp what our office was all about. The desk trainer shouted at him and on one occasion actually struck him, barking that he wasn't listening to a word she said. The Training Officer was called in and there was no confidentiality; we all heard what they thought of Graham.

After about three weeks of this, one day Graham didn't appear for work. Since he lived alone, the Welfare Officer was despatched to his home. She found him dead on the floor and involved the police. It transpired that Graham had had a brain tumour without knowing anything about it. When this news broke in our section, I watched for any kind of repentance from either the desk trainer or the Training Officer, and of course there was none.

"How were we supposed to know if he didn't?" was their attitude. Are people born bullies?

There was much more I observed, while avoiding becoming involved, many tears I helped to wipe away over the years, caused by nastiness for its own sake and most commonly by jealousy.

Two more marriages…

Eventually I met a nice man I thought I could live with, and married again. I moved about 100 miles away and was very happy.

Meanwhile Roly had also married. His wife was what I called a manager. She appeared to make all the decisions and Roly was content to let her do so. I wondered if that was the reason for the marriage, if maybe he was unable or unwilling to make decisions for himself, but to be fair he seemed happy with the arrangement.

We had nothing in common, this woman and I. I tried to get along with her but found no subject we could talk about. She resented me from the beginning and cut me out of their lives as much as she could. I accepted this and left them alone.

I kept in touch with my mother and phoned her regularly. I could tell when she was getting to the end of her patience with Father and I would travel back and take her out for the day. This seemed to help her, and if he took it out on her later she did not tell me so.

I do remember on one of these occasions asking her if he had ever physically abused her. She hesitated before she said "No".

One example of how he treated her was this. They had moved to sheltered accommodation as Mum became more disabled with arthritis. She did not want to leave the cottage they had lived in since he retired, but it was his decision of course. He had a nameplate made for the sheltered flat, with *his* name only on it. So typical.

Another time she rang me in some distress. We had as a family been to a local hotel to celebrate Mother's 80th birthday. We all had an input, so the expense was shared.

When they got home afterwards Father had a raging tantrum because she hadn't told us all that he had paid for a new dress for her for the special day. He then refused to speak to her at all.

My mother and I became very close in her last few years, and that is something I still treasure.

…and a death

Three years after this Mother became ill, and after a longish spell in hospital it was clear that she would not get better. My husband and I went down to visit her every other day for the few weeks after they told us she would not recover. She was so patient. The day they told her she wouldn't be going home, we were all there – my father, my husband and I, both my children, now grown up, Roly and his wife.

Before they moved her to her own private room, she asked me to give her ten minutes. Though I was utterly shocked and bereft, I acted normally and sat with her. She took my wrist in her hand and held on tightly.

"I want your promise," she said.

"Anything," I replied.

"I want you to promise you will see to your father." She was still gripping me like a vice.

I was horrified. I had had no intention of seeing to my father.

"I know what I'm asking," she said, "I do realise how you feel."

I could not answer for a few minutes. In the end I said, "I promise I will do the best I can."

She let me go. "That's good enough," she said, and she sank back on her pillows, "because you're the strong one."

I was amazed. "Oh no, I've only been strong because of you," I protested.

She looked straight at me, although her sight was poor by then.

"You're wrong. You're stronger than you know."

With that the rest of the family appeared. I treasure what she said, and it has meant more to me than any of his taunts.

We went to see her every other day for the few weeks before she died. I was not with her when she died, but Father was. He rang me and we went to him immediately. I was stunned, partly with grief but partly at the sight of him. He was utterly broken.

* * *

I should have realised at once that Father would need

all my sympathy and attention, regardless of my own indescribable grief. He met me with an envelope thrust into my hands. My mother's rings. My resolution to be strong was shattered instantly. I did my best but it was so hard.

He then asked me to unpack her bag, which the hospital had sent back. I was fine until I got to her glasses, which she wore all the time, and I was heartbroken. My husband helped me, but it was a sorry time and Father demanded and expected all the attention.

I must now bring in Rusty, my parents' minister, a very unusual man of the church, thought much of by Father, a devout Christian, and also by my mother, who "had her doubts" about God.

All through her final illness, Rusty visited her almost daily, whenever he could spare the time. I do not know what passed between them, but she died serene and accepting, in what is known as a state of grace. I believe this was at least partly due to Rusty.

We stayed the night, as next day her funeral had to be arranged. The practicalities were seen to by my brother's cold-hearted wife, "to save me the bother". But I was determined to arrange the service with Rusty without interference.

We waited for Rusty, my husband and I, Roly and his

wife, and of course Father. He was silent and not paying attention to what was going on, and Roly's wife (I can't even give her a name) began to ask me odd questions, implying I was a thief, a liar, a bad mother, a disgrace of a grandparent and no friend of anybody. It appeared she had been in touch with my mother's adopted sister Kate, and they had torn me to pieces with their lies and viciousness. Two of a kind they were.

I asked her why she was asking me all these loaded questions and she said, "Oh, no reason". Roly of course said nothing at all. By then I could recognise bullying in a very short time. Luckily, Rusty appeared and I got my own way with the arrangements.

On the day of the funeral, we travelled down early, picking up my daughter on the way. Because I had not been with my mother when she died, I wanted to see her one last time, and I had arranged this with the undertakers. It was a terrible mistake. I had never seen a dead person before, and this was not her. And if she wasn't there, inside the body, she wasn't anywhere, and I was not ready for that.

We got through the service and all that followed, then went back home with Father, who appeared to be helpless and not wanting to be left alone. I arranged for

Roly's wife to be in the company of my husband, briefly, and I had asked him to tell her a few home truths, which he was pleased to do. No one ever bullied him. I myself was the last to leave Father that day, in keeping with my promise to my mother.

CHAPTER SEVEN

The months that followed were the biggest test of patience I have ever known. Father seemed to have gone mad, or at least unbalanced. Fawned on and cosseted by women all his life, he now wanted attention all the time. Sometimes he would meet some woman he knew and she would give him a sympathetic hug. He took this as a green light and began to hug and kiss them back. Once he even called on one of them when her husband was out and launched himself at her. She threatened him with the police and he left. He even had the cheek to tell me about it.

He sent north to an old girlfriend, also over 80, and her daughter brought her to visit. He sent the daughter out and again embraced this poor woman till she shouted for help. And again he told me. I was horrified. Also, he would regale me with stories of his conquests over his whole life, both before and after he married my mother. It was all made up, I am sure, but even so, this was not what I wanted to hear.

He had a wonderful lady doctor, also my mother's GP, who foolishly asked him to call her by her first name. He told me this meant she fancied him, and when he reported this to me I realised I had to do something.

I wrote to Rusty. Bless him, he rang me with words of supreme comfort. He would set things right and I was not to worry. He seemed to know more about our family than a minister would. Perhaps my mother had told him, I wondered? He said to me, "Your father is carrying a burden of guilt none of us should envy".

He had contacted the doctor, and Father had been transferred to another GP, a young man. Rusty said that his bizarre behaviour was not at all uncommon in bereaved men. I reckoned that was a reason but not an excuse, but there remained my promise.

Banished

Twice we had him to stay for a couple of days, a very

difficult time for us. The second time was the first Christmas without her. I had done everything I could to make it special, all his favourite things to eat and so on. He complained about absolutely everything. During the meal I had had enough and broke down. After all, it was *my* first Christmas without her too. My husband hit the roof. "Pack your bags," he roared, "you're going home. Right now, without the meal." For once I didn't stop him.

And so we took him home, and when we got back I tore down the Christmas tree and all the cards and packed it all away. He never came to stay again.

We had peace after that for a time, as he was now attended by a housekeeper. She flattered him, the right thing to do, and he plied her with money, so she kept his house, taking the pressure off me. We went to see him once a fortnight, with my daughter, and did whatever he needed done. We took him shopping while he was able, and he sometimes took us out for a meal. I know that Roly also visited him every two weeks although he was still working. I admired him for that, and still do.

One memorable day I nearly killed him.

He was in his small kitchen and I went in to make tea. Somehow the conversation got around to my mother's sister Kate being illegitimate, as my mother had been. He actually said about my mother, "But you know, in all the years I have known her, I never once held it against her."

I could not believe my ears. This was a man with a good degree and a fine brain. I was standing beside an open drawer with knives in it. My hand went into the drawer, and I could almost feel the knife going into him. I asked him to say it again, and he did. I tottered into the other room and said, "I will be in the car".

My husband and daughter were amazed. "What's up?" he asked.

I couldn't answer. In tears, I fled to the car and locked myself in. They came out in a minute, and I could not for the life of me tell them what he had said.

I cried all the way home, for my poor mother whom he had thought so little of, for his pitiful ignorance and feelings of superiority, for the shaming knowledge that he was my father, and for all the kindness we had shown him in his bereavement, regardless of our own grief.

It was several weeks before I could speak to him on the phone, and to his dying day he had no idea why I had been upset.

Then his health began to fail and it became more of an effort to visit him. He had carers in to get him up and put him to bed, and eventually he was hospitalised. I had power of attorney, which at least told me how much he had given to his housekeeper.

We managed to find him a nursing home not too far away, and Roly, my daughter and I cleared his flat. Even in the nursing home, he did not behave himself. We would go and visit once a week or so, but by now my husband would not go near him. One day the lady in charge asked to see us and my daughter and I went in, fearing the worst. One of the carers was black and another obviously foreign, Central European I think. He had made a racist remark to each of them and she had had to tell him off.

I laughed. "I could have warned you he would," I said to her, "You can beat him with a stick for all I care."

She was relieved.

Not long after that, she sent for us one day, as he was deteriorating fast. We all appeared that afternoon, Roly, my husband, our daughter and me, and my cousin Mags, who still thought the world of him and called him "The Chief." We said our goodbyes and to my utter amazement I was inconsolable, as was Roly.

I should very much like to know why we were not completely jubilant, but that's how it was. We gave him a splendid funeral, and Rusty did him proud. I wept throughout, and still I do not know why.

Searching for answers

While the verbal and physical abuse was going on, right through childhood and teenage years, I do not remember wondering where it came from, how he had become such a monster. Since his death, I have increasingly questioned the origins of his control mania. Having read numerous books and articles on psychology, and even done a psychology course with the Open University, I am still no further forward.

He was born, the fifth child and the fourth son, in 1915 on a croft in the far north of Scotland. Life was hard and there was not much in the way of luxury. All his brothers resembled their mother, Mary; only he looked anything like his father, James. Mary was gentle and obedient, luckily, for James was not. He was hard on his children and bullied his wife. By all accounts, he was a monster. If he was less than pleased with his dinner, he threw it, plate and all, to the floor or hurled it at whoever was nearest, or so I have been told.

Despite the hardness of their early lives, Father and

his brothers thrived and either went into farming on their own, or worked at other occupations, all successfully. Father was the only one to go on to further education, I am not sure why. He was little short of brilliant at school and obtained bursaries which helped to see him through his degree financially.

When he took my mother home the first time, before they were married, his father was hostile to her openly. He told her bluntly that his son should marry a local girl. She wondered if it was because she was illegitimate. After they married, when I was a baby, he took her there again, and my grandfather was even more antagonistic to Mother. She put up with it, helped by Mary, who made her feel welcome.

Also, when he was first a student in Edinburgh, he stayed briefly with his cousin Ella. She also took against my mother, for the same reason. It could not be the illegitimacy, therefore, because this Ella also had a daughter out of wedlock.

Perhaps both of these relations of Father's looking down on her made him see her as inferior? Maybe his physical resemblance to his father also reflected a character likeness, and he was basically a cruel taskmaster, unlike his brothers, who had a great deal of their mother's gentleness.

During the war, when I was very small, Ella's daughter Isa used to come in the school holidays to stay with us. She was maybe fourteen or fifteen, great fun and singing all the current popular songs to us ('Lay That Pistol Down, Babe'). Ella had married and had a son and I wonder now if Isa needed to escape her stepfather. My mother hinted as much, many years later. We were not the only ones to be bullied. Ella also would visit, and pick fault wherever she could. My mother was never good enough, it seemed.

It could have been any of these things, or perhaps it was none of them. Maybe bullies are just born that way.

I believe now that the army had a lot to do with it. As teaching was a reserved occupation, I am at a loss to understand why he volunteered in 1940, though I do know his heart was never in teaching.

There were certain questions he would always answer about the army, and some he would not. He had applied for a commission, based on his very good degree from Edinburgh University, but he failed the interview. He would never discuss this and I do not understand how he came to fail. I can only assume snobbery came into it and he was from poor crofters, so that was enough.

But I will say this for him: he went in as a gunner, and

in quick time he rose to sergeant. He was posted to the Mediterranean conflict, Italy, Sicily, Yugoslavia and Greece. As a classics student this suited him very well. He had an aptitude for languages and enjoyed learning the basics of the local language wherever he was posted.

One of his unit must have had a camera, for there are photos of him in shorts, smiling and laughing and enjoying it all. There was no direct killing, although their ack-ack guns brought down many a plane. They seemed to have plenty of time off and there was enough food.

He often spoke of his army days. As a classics scholar he revelled in the ancient buildings of Greece and Italy. He told me once that they had been stationed near Rome and he had gone into the city to see the sights. It was a blistering hot day. He came upon the Coliseum, which at that time was not commercialised as it is today. He went inside, thrilled to be in the place he had read so much about. When he entered the catacombs the air became icy cold. He could only stay for a few minutes, it was so freezing, although it was open to the sky. Although he was not an imaginative man, he was taken aback. So was I, until I visited the Coliseum myself one day. I felt ill as soon as I went inside, and soon had to come out, where I was fine again. Bad, bad doings in there once, to leave such unpleasant vibes behind after all this time.

The patriots in all the Mediterranean countries made our army lads very welcome, from what I gather, and they had a not altogether difficult war. When the war in Europe ended, Father was drafted into the Education Corps, being a qualified teacher, and taught prisoners of war English. So his war was mostly being in charge, and he had got very used to that.

How extremely unsettling it must have been for all the soldiers coming home to shortages and little money. He said he had learned to sleep on concrete floors or hard chairs, and never known exactly what he was being asked to eat, but they were not rationed, as we at home were.

I suppose they expected a hero's welcome home, but we had nothing to give them, as we had been hard put to it to feed ourselves. I do not remember many overweight people at that time!

Accustomed to being mostly in the warm open air and eating oranges etc. from wayside trees, it must have come hard to have no fruit or luxuries when they came home.

Until the day he died, Father spoke often about his time in the army as a great adventure. Latterly, although he was becoming frail and forgetful, his memories of the war never faded. I remember trying to cheer him up when he became ill by asking him, "How did Greece become involved in the war?" Twenty minutes later he was still talking, and it all made sense.

We gave him a party on his ninetieth birthday. I managed to get him a cake with the Royal Artillery badge on top. We did it all, invitations, hiring the lounge, making food and clearing up. He took it all for granted, as he always did. Of course he was the centre of attention that day, which was what he enjoyed most.

Since he died, I have noticed that many books have been written about child abuse, although I cannot bring myself to read them. Most seem to be about sexual abuse, which (though I may have blanked it) did not happen to me, but there have been many, many families destroyed by cruelty. We are not alone.

★ ★ ★

I do not hate him. I was full of anger for a long time, but if I feel anything now, it is pity. Pity for the confused, frustrated, striving man he was.

At the end of his life, he often told me he loved me and had always been proud of me. I was very uncomfortable with this. He wanted me to say I loved him, but I could not. Even on that last day, when I knew I would not see him again, I could not say it.

To this day, I have difficulty accepting praise of any kind, from anybody. Writing this all down has helped me to believe in myself. I am working on *liking* myself, and now have hope that that will happen.

Roly, like me, has made a success of his chosen career. In the man he is now, well-liked by those who know him, I see nothing of the brutally-abused little boy he was. He will not talk to me about the abuse, though memories are hard to erase and who knows what he thinks.

I feared my father once, but now I am free.

ND - #0519 - 270225 - C0 - 203/127/8 - PB - 9781861514660 - Matt Lamination